SPECIAL NEEDS *in the early years*

CW00348430

Meeting special needs in early years settings

SEN Co-ordinator's handbook

...LE OF SENCO ● HOW TO WRITE AN SEN POLICY ● STAFF TRAINING ● WORKING WITH OTHER PROFESSIONALS

DR HANNAH MORTIMER

Author
Dr Hannah Mortimer

Editor
Victoria Lee

Assistant Editor
Aileen Lalor

Series Designers
Sarah Rock/Anna Oliwa

Designer
Erik Ivens

Illustrations
Shelagh McNicholas

Cover artwork
Claire Henley

Acknowledgements
The publishers would like to thank **Disability Equality in Education** for the use of
material based on a Venn diagram from *Inclusion in the early years: DEE Course Book* by
Richard Rieser and Christine O'Mahony © Richard Rieser and Christine O'Mahony (2001,
Disability Equality in Education)

Text © 2004, Hannah Mortimer
© 2004, Scholastic Ltd

Designed using Adobe InDesign
Published by Scholastic Ltd, Villiers House,
Clarendon Avenue, Leamington Spa, Warwickshire CV32 5PR

Visit our website at www.scholastic.co.uk

Printed by Bell and Bain Ltd, Glasgow
1 2 3 4 5 6 7 8 9 0   4 5 6 7 8 9 0 1 2 3

Alice Kheiraki

SEN Co-ordinator's Handbook

Alice Kheirabi

SEN Co-ordinator's Handbook

INTRODUCTION

In many early years settings, there will be children with SEN. This book provides SENCOs with advice on how to meet the requirements of the Code of Practice and most importantly, how to best support children, parents, carers and colleagues.

Aims of the series

A revised Code of Practice for the identification and assessment of special educational needs has been published by the DfES. There are also new guidelines for providing day care and for including children with disabilities. This series aims to provide suggestions to early years practitioners on how to meet and monitor special educational needs (SEN) under the new guidelines. In addition, the QCA Early Learning Goals emphasise the key role that early years educators play in identifying needs and responding quickly to them.

Within this *Special Needs in the Early Years* series, there are already eight books on helping children with most kinds of special need:
- behavioural and emotional difficulties
- speech and language difficulties
- learning difficulties
- physical and co-ordination difficulties
- autistic spectrum difficulties
- medical difficulties
- sensory difficulties.

There is also a *Special Needs Handbook* with general information to will help you meet all the special educational needs in your setting.

A further two books now complement this series: *SENCO's handbook – supporting colleagues in early years settings* and *The Essential A–Z Guide to Special Needs.*

Whereas the first eight books in the series provided general information about SEN, this book focuses on what the special educational needs co-ordinator (or 'SENCO') needs to know, and how to pass on that knowledge to others. The tenth book in the series, *The Essential A–Z Guide of Special Needs*, has been specifically written for early years educators themselves and can be a useful tool for the SENCO to pass on to those actually working with the children with SEN.

Who this book is for

This book is for SENCOs and Area SENCOs. These people now have new roles and responsibilities and this book will support them in passing on skills and information about SEN to the colleagues they are

supporting. It will also be of interest to early years staff who work in a range of different settings – teachers, early years support staff, managers and trainers.

Each registered setting is required to appoint a SENCO who will act as the contact point for all SEN matters. Many SENCOs are also taking on a new role in ensuring equal opportunities within their settings. There are now new requirements for SENCOs to support their colleagues in meeting SEN. The SENCO's handbook will provide SENCOs with both the general information and the practical suggestions for fulfilling their new roles.

How to use the book

You will find it useful to skim through the whole book, to identify where you feel colleagues need more support, and then to focus on those chapters which are useful for your setting. The first two chapters cover the role of the SENCO and how to write an inclusive SEN policy; the contents will be very familiar to those of you already in post but are a useful introduction for:

- newly appointed SENCOs,
- newly registered settings,
- small settings about to welcome a child with SEN for the first time,
- SENCOs who feel they need more reassurance and confidence.

Next follow two chapters on new legislation and guidance – the SEN Disability Act and your new role in ensuring equal opportunities.

You will probably already be familiar with assessing SEN and setting individual education plans (IEPs) and there is full information in the *Special Needs Handbook* by Hannah Mortimer (Scholastic). Chapter 5 of this book has suggestions for helping colleagues develop their own skills and for keeping the process child-centred. The next chapters cover your role in arranging meetings and reviews and working with parents, carers and other professionals. Chapter 9 contains ideas for supporting colleagues in managing difficult behaviour (you will find fuller information in the book *Managing Children's Behaviour* from Scholastic's *Early Years Training and Management* series). The last chapter helps you to arrange training events for colleagues and the photocopiables that follow can be used as handouts. The last two photocopiables are an evaluation form for the training you offer and a resource list for your colleagues to keep.

Legal requirements

You will find a fuller picture of the legal framework for meeting SEN in the *Special Needs Handbook* by Hannah Mortimer (Scholastic). All registered early years settings are required to 'have regard to' The SEN Code of Practice. It recommends that schools and early years providers should identify children's needs and take action to meet those needs as

early as possible, working with parents and carers. The aim is to enable all pupils with SEN to reach their full potential, to be included fully in their school communities and to make a successful transition to adulthood. The Code gives guidance to schools and early years providers, but it does not tell them what they must do in every case.

It is recognised that good practice can take many forms, and early years providers are encouraged to adopt a flexible and graduated response to the SEN of individual children. This approach recognises that there is a continuum of SEN and, where necessary, brings increasing specialist expertise on board if the child is experiencing continuing difficulties. Once a child's SEN have been identified, the providers should intervene through 'Early Years Action'. This intervention is co-ordinated by one person within the setting who has been designated as the SENCO. However, each adult in the setting shares the responsibility of intervening to support the child. This is the one of the greatest challenges for SENCOs – how to pass knowledge and expertise on to those actually working with the children concerned.

When reviewing the child's progress and the help he or she is receiving, the SENCO might decide to seek alternative approaches to learning through the support of the outside support services. These interventions are known as 'Early Years Action Plus'. Early Years Action Plus is characterised by the involvement of specialists from outside the setting. For a very few children, the help provided by Early Years Action Plus will still not be sufficient to ensure satisfactory progress. The SENCO, external professional and parents and carers may then decide to ask the LEA to consider carrying out a statutory assessment of the child's SEN. These children may go on to receive 'statements' of SEN and, though the SEN are now monitored by the local education authority (LEA), the SENCO continues to play a role in co-ordinating the SEN provision for these children within the setting.

Providing education and care

Registered early years providers are also expected to deliver this broad and balanced curriculum across six 'Areas of Learning' as defined in the Early Learning Goals and the Curriculum Guidance for the Foundation Stage (QCA 2000). Defining a set of Early Learning Goals which most children will have attained by the end of the Foundation Stage (the end of their reception year) has helped to ensure that nursery education is of good quality and is a sound preparation for later schooling. In order to ensure this, registered early years providers are required to have their

educational provision inspected regularly. One of the areas inspected is how effectively staff can identify, support and monitor the needs of the children with SEN in the setting. Inevitably, it is the SENCO who co-ordinates the information on SEN ready for inspection, and this book should put you in a better position to meet your obligations.

The 'Full Day Care National Standards' (ref DfES 0488/2001) contain guidance on the standards that settings should aim for in all aspects of childcare including meeting SEN and the provision of equal opportunities. Quite often, it is the SENCO in the setting who is also given the role of being the contact person for equal opportunities. That is why you will find a chapter in this book about equal opportunities and inclusion as well as SEN issues and conditions.

Supporting colleagues

Perhaps this introduces the greatest challenge to any early years SENCO. Each of your colleagues will have a unique combination of past experiences and training, ranging from none at all, through experiences of parenthood, to graduate teaching status. Each will also bring their own levels of confidence or uncertainty. Yet it is their responsibility, and not the SENCO's, to meet the everyday SEN of the children concerned. We now know that the emotional aspects of learning are very important to adults – you will read more about these in Chapter 10. Any learning process involves change; something is invariably added or taken away. Such 'unlearning' can lead to fear, anxiety and resistance for the learner. Therefore, your colleagues will learn best if the learning environment is kept informal and non-threatening, and steps are taken to encourage the learner, inspire confidence, and 'license' the learner to feel secure enough to 'have a go' with the new approaches. An informality of approach and the need for the trainer to inspire confidence in the learner should be key features of SENCO training and support. This book aims to provide you with just those skills – to inform, to support and to enthuse your colleagues effectively so that the children benefit and become fully included.

ROLE OF THE SENCO

This chapter explains what a special educational needs co-ordinator is supposed to do, how other staff are involved and the way that the SENCO's role fits in with the latest legislation on SEN and disabilities.

Recent developments

Government guidance has made it clear that there should be a special educational needs co-ordinator (SENCO) in every registered early years setting. The SEN Code of Practice states that the provision for children with special educational needs is a matter for everyone in the setting. Of course, the setting's headteacher or manager and the SENCO have important responsibilities, but so do all other members of staff. In practice, the division of day-to-day responsibilities is a matter for individual settings, and you will need to find the right way of delegating the responsibility which works for your setting.

The planning guidance also asked Early Years Development and Childcare Partnerships (EYDCPs) and now Sure Start Partnerships, to plan how to improve SEN support for their early years settings. They were also charged with establishing networks of Area SENCOs to support settings, giving early identification of SEN and access to appropriate specialist services. Each setting was asked to identify and train a SENCO to link with a new network of Area SENCOs who will provide advice and support. The Government set out to put in place a network of Area SENCOs, with a target ratio of one Area SENCO to twenty non-maintained settings delivering funded early education, by 2004. The idea is that this should lead to better outcomes for children and reduce the need for costly intervention later. At about the same time, the Government introduced targets for children with SEN in day care services. Area SENCOs are selected because of their competence to advise settings on SEN and equal opportunities issues, drawing on the expertise of school SENCOs, special schools, local projects and other agencies. They usually have qualified teacher status and must have wide experience as a setting-based SENCO.

Roles and responsibilities

The main responsibility of a setting-based SENCO is for the everyday operation of SEN policy (Chapter 2) and this might include:
● making sure that the setting sets up appropriate procedures for working with and including disabled children and those with other forms of SEN.
● working with other staff and parents/carers on producing a written SEN policy.
● co-ordinating provision for children with SEN within their setting and making sure that each child's SEN are being met.
● making sure that the needs of disabled children and those with

other forms of SEN are being included in all aspects of the setting's planning and practice.

● making sure that all staff have an understanding of the setting's practice in relation to disabled children and those with other forms of SEN, and that there is consistency and continuity in the way it is carried out.

● supporting staff in making observations and in setting appropriate targets for meeting individual children's needs and entitlements, by ensuring that appropriate IEPs are in place.

● contributing to statutory assessments and reviews for children who have statements.

You do not need to be a specialist or an expert straight away. You simply need to be interested, committed to including the children with SEN, willing to gather and store information in a way which makes it usable, and able to support other staff in what they are doing to meet SEN, seeking further advice and support where necessary. At first you will find yourself asking more questions than you can answer, but day by day, child by child, you will develop your confidence, skills and knowledge.

Acting as a resource

SENCOs fulfil a key role in identifying children in need of additional support and in helping settings improve access and achieve inclusion. The planning guidance for Early Years Development and Childcare Partnerships (EYDCPs) allowed three days relevant training by 2004 for every one of those SENCOs. The idea is that, once trained in basic knowledge of SEN issues, SENCOs will be in a position to support and train their colleagues to meet their new responsibilities. The SENCO is usually also the one who is responsible for establishing and implementing the setting's equal opportunities policy (Chapter 4).

Assessment and early intervention

● SENCOs should act as a contact for other members of staff on training and on interpreting the Code of Practice. You will find

plenty of ideas throughout this book.

● They should support them in identifying and meeting the SEN of children within the setting. In other words, they should help colleagues work out which children's needs cannot be met through the differentiation and flexibility available in the setting (and in early years, these are already key features in educating very young children) and therefore need approaches which are additional or different.

● They must oversee records kept on individual children's SEN. There will probably be a file, perhaps with copies of any assessments, observations, IEPs,

minutes of review meetings, parent/carer letters and examples of the child's achievements and progress.

● SENCOs should put other members of staff in touch with relevant SEN training so that they can identify and plan for any SEN as early as possible. This is likely to be available through the local Sure Start Partnership or LEA.

● Do not be put off if you feel that you have no expertise in identifying specific conditions (such as AD/HD or dyspraxia). You are already experts in how young children learn and play and in the Foundation Stage curriculum. Use your SEN knowledge to help staff to develop their existing methods of observation and assessment (as used for all the children) so that you can also identify those children who are not accessing the curriculum. You might decide to organise your resources in a way which helps all children access the six different Areas of Learning – this would be the inclusive way of looking at your assessment and planning. You will find more ideas in Chapter 5.

Contact with parents and carers

● SENCOs have an important role in developing and maintaining relationships in order to ensure effective liaison with parents/carers.

● Although it may not be the SENCO's direct responsibility to liaise with every parent or carer of a child with SEN, he or she must ensure that it happens as constructively and effectively as possible.

● The SENCO should also be responsible for supporting staff in meetings or reviews with parents/carers, and in setting appropriate targets, review dates and times.

● The SENCO should ensure that parents/carers of children with SEN are kept informed and are consulted throughout.

● You will find ideas and suggestions about working with families in Chapter 7.

Links with other professionals

● The SENCO should take responsibility for the setting's liaison with external agencies, including the local authority educational psychology service, to gain information, advice or support in relation to disability and SEN issues.

● The SENCO should act as a first point of contact on SEN for the LEA, Health Services, Social Services and others.

● He or she should seek outside advice and support if necessary, for children already in the setting or about to join it.

● There are ideas and more information about the outside professionals who can support you in Chapter 8.

Keeping records

In most settings, the SENCO will have decided to maintain an SEN register or equivalent recording system. Although the SEN Code of Practice does not make this obligatory, it does seem to make sense to have a list of all the children who need something 'additional' or 'different' to meet their educational needs. In this way, you can track what is being done and when it needs to be reviewed. This system

could usefully include the names of all children in the setting who have been identified as having SEN, whether their needs are being monitored as Early Years Action, Early Years Action Plus or through a statement of SEN. It could also include the date of the next review of the individual education plan (IEP).

The SENCO also needs to co-ordinate and keep on file all information and correspondence on children with SEN, and make sure each individual child on the SEN register has a file. Although this file should be stored confidentially, there will be other professionals in the setting who need to have access to it. If you are meeting SEN inclusively, you will be making sure that parents and carers have copies of or access to what is in the file. Sometimes there might be occasions when you have access to confidential medical information or child protection reports which would be more appropriately stored in a locked cabinet, separate from the day-to-day documentation.

Training others

The SENCO can make a significant contribution to staff professional development by keeping up-to-date with any national or local developments on provision for children with SEN.

● Make sure that relevant information is efficiently passed on to staff and management.
● Identify the individual training needs of staff in relation to SEN and disability and plan suitable training or support for them.
● You will find ideas in Chapter 10 for organising and running your own training for staff.
● Never assume that an outsider can do this better than you – you are the expert on how SEN are met in your setting and are in the best position to pitch training and information at just the right level for the staff. You can also make sure that the training is possible, practical and productive.

Additional reading

● There are fuller descriptions of much of this terminology in the *Special Needs Handbook* by Hannah Mortimer (Scholastic) and a general introduction to a wide range of SEN in the other books in this series (see page 5).
● The Pre-school Learning Alliance (69 Kings Cross Road, London WC1X 9LL, www.pre-school.org.uk) has published a book, *The role of the SENCO in pre-school settings*.
● *Special needs in early years settings – A guide for practitioners* by Collette Drifte (David Fulton Publishers).
● *How to survive and succeed as a SENCO in the primary school* by Veronica Birkett (LDA).

WRITING AN INCLUSIVE SEN POLICY

This chapter explains how best to write your inclusive SEN policy, keeping it practical and workable and with an awareness of legislation and national policy.

What inclusion means

All registered early years settings should have an SEN policy. What would an inclusive SEN policy look like?

● Your policy should make it clear that your group welcomes all children whatever their individual needs or abilities.

● This should be clearly stated in any parents'/carers' handbooks and literature.

● If your setting is registered to receive Government funding, staff must meet the requirements of the SEN Code of Practice (page 6).

● Staff members should have the opportunities to take up training in both special needs and early years practice.

● Your Foundation Stage curriculum planning should be suitable for all children.

● There should be opportunities for all children to feel successful in each learning situation.

● You should develop ways of sharing observations and planning with parents and carers.

● You should try to use methods of communication which include everyone, and which can be used between children (for example, using sign language or more than one language within your setting).

● You need to be prepared to be flexible and change what you are doing in order to meet a particular child's needs.

● You need to involve professionals from outside agencies when necessary and to include them in your planning.

● All the staff should work and plan together to meet any special educational needs, with the support of the SENCO.

● Planning for SEN should not be seen as the entire responsibility of the SENCO.

● You should be able to provide families with the names and contact details of relevant support services.

Active policy making

There are several national policies that should influence the policies that you write for your setting:

● the National Childcare Strategy – this is the strategy that created new funded places for three and four-year-olds.

● the revision of the SEN Code of Practice – this was the guidance that amended the systems for monitoring SEN and brought parents/carers and inclusion more firmly on board.

● The Curriculum Review – this includes the changes in what children should learn in the early years, including the Foundation Stage curriculum.

● The review of regulation and inspection – this includes the introduction of inspections for childcare and education, ensuring quality of provision.
● Training review – the whole status of childcare and early education has been raised in recent years with a more co-ordinated training structure.

The SENCO is likely to lead the writing and reviewing of the SEN policy. This need not be as daunting as it sounds because the best policies are simply maps which will help us to travel from where we are now to where we want to be. In other words, policy making should be an active and practical process.

What the policy should contain

Your policy should contain the following information.
● It should begin with a short summary of the beliefs shared by staff regarding children who have SEN. You might, for example, say that you want all children to be entitled to a broad, balanced and purposeful early years curriculum and that you will work with parents, carers and agencies in order to achieve this. The policy should go on to say how you will do this. How will you:
  – decide which children need help and what you will do about it?
  – monitor, record and evaluate all children's progress and identify, assess and review any special needs?
  – provide additional resources and support for children with SEN? publish admissions arrangements with relation to children who have SEN?
  – consider complaints about SEN provision within the setting?
● Your policy should provide information on the name of the setting's member of staff with responsibility for the day-to-day operation of the SEN policy (usually the SENCO).
● It should list any SEN expertise and qualifications of the staff within the setting.
● It should explain how you will all obtain training on SEN.
● What resources for supporting SEN are already available within the setting?
● Who are your local support services, and how do you access them if you need to?

You will find a possible format on page 49 which can be shared with colleagues and used to develop or review your SEN policy.

Consulting with others

Once you have developed an SEN policy for your setting, it is helpful to share it with any visiting professional who might be able to give you practical advice on how to make sure that your policy is inclusive. Find the opportunity to share it with parents and carers and seek their views at each stage of your policy making process. Sometimes, you need to invest time and attention to make sure that you have parents and carers 'on board' with your inclusive policy. Their views on inclusion still vary widely across the country, with

some eloquent and powerful voices towards inclusion for all, and also some fearful whispers about what inclusion might actually mean for their disabled child. Will the level of care be the same? Will the child be 'protected'? Will the right resources and support be provided? It will only be through designing, properly resourcing and successfully implementing inclusion that everyone feels reassured that it can work for all.

Keeping it practical

Here are some ways in which you can encourage making play and learning approaches accessible for all children wherever possible. This is the kind of information you can include in your policy.

● Try not to have 'special' activities for 'special' children or to buy plenty of 'special needs' equipment as this does not help the development of an inclusive provision.

● Often, an activity can be changed in some way rather than excluding certain children from it because they cannot fit in with it. Flexible approaches and adaptable timetables and routines make this much easier and more practical.

● Outdoor play areas need to contain quiet, sheltered spaces as well as busy, active areas.

● Indoors, tables and equipment need to be at adjustable heights and floor spaces should be comfortable and safe to play on.

● Acoustics can be softened with soft surfaces, cushions, carpets and curtains, making it easier for everyone to hear clearly.

● Story times can be kept concrete by using props and visual aids.

● Communication can be enhanced by making sure that all adults are familiar with any communication system used by the children, such as sign language or if English is not their first language.

● Children can also have a communication book with pictures or text showing how they make their needs known.

● Make use of colours, textures and smells to encourage different senses and to develop sensory play.

● Look for ways of making tools and equipment easy to handle by all children, such as wrapping foam padding around paintbrush handles to make them easier to hold or using non-slip mats to hold small toys in position.

● Throughout the curriculum, look out for materials, pictures and books that contain positive images of disabled people and people with special needs.

Monitoring and review

Your setting's SEN policy needs to be brought up to date whenever there is new legislation. This means that it will have been updated

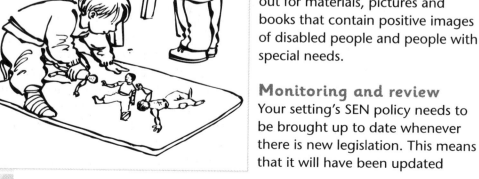

following the new SEN Code of Practice in 2001 and the Disability Rights Commission Code of Practice in late 2002. It should be reviewed annually in any case. You should involve colleagues in discussions about how effective the policy has been and how well it is leading to the progress of children who have SEN. The day-to-day operation of the SEN policy is the role of the setting's special educational needs co-ordinator or 'SENCO'. It is usually helpful to use an annual parents'/carers', management or governors' meeting to regularly review the SEN policy and to suggest any changes that need to be made in light of new guidance.

In order to provide information for your policy review, it is helpful to plan a 'practice audit' first. This means gathering information about where the service is at the moment.
- Are there any disabled children using the service?
- Is the environment inclusive?
- What are your strengths and weaknesses?
- What special equipment/staff/adaptations does your service have?
- Do you take into account the needs of disabled children in any changes in practice or approach as a result of new initiatives?

Checklist – how good is our SEN policy?

Do the staff and management in your setting have:
- Commitment to an equal opportunities philosophy and approach?
- A shared responsibility to address equal opportunities in a consistent manner?

Have the staff and management in your setting:
- Identified any low cost changes that can be made in the next year to improve access and arrangements?
- Consulted with disabled users of buildings (staff/children/parents/carers) about any small changes to arrangements which might be helpful?
- Ensured the display of materials that reflect a positive image of disabled people and children?

Do the staff and management in your setting:
- Encourage all children to develop a positive sense of self image and a pride in their own identity?
- Encourage disabled children to accept challenge and participate in a wide range of activities?
- Have equally high expectations of all children and take steps to ensure that they can take sensible risks?
- Know where to get guidance and support when necessary?
- Have links with community professionals for direct help or training in relation to care needed by individual children?

This checklist has been adapted from the very practical book All Together – how to provide inclusive services for young disabled children and their families, by Mary Dickins with Judy Denziloe (2nd edition, National Children's Bureau).

THE SEN DISABILITY ACT

This chapter explains how the Disability Discrimination Act and the SEN Disability Act should affect the way you treat children with SEN or other disabilities in your setting, and how to make sure your curriculum is accessible to all.

A new Act

The Disability Discrimination Act 1995 (DDA) brought in new legal measures to clarify disabled people's rights in terms of employment, obtaining goods and services, buying or renting land or property and transport. The Act was amended to cover the requirements on establishments which provide education and day care for children and this formed the Special Educational Need and Disability Act (SENDA) 2001. These are the main points:

● Under the Act, a disabled person has 'a physical or mental impairment, which has an effect on his or her ability to carry out normal day to day activities. That effect must be substantial (not trivial or minor), adverse and long-term'.

● Many children who are disabled will have SEN and many who have SEN will be disabled in some way, so there is overlap.

● Settings are also required to overcome physical features which impede access to a service and from late 2004 may have to make other adjustments to the physical environment to overcome physical barriers to access.

● You cannot refuse a service (such as early years education), offer a worse standard of service or offer a service on worse terms to a disabled child or person unless you can offer a 'justification'. This is called the 'less favourable treatment' duty. Even if you can offer justification, you will be expected to demonstrate that you are planning ahead to improve access and inclusion in the future.

● You need to plan 'reasonable adjustments' for disabled children. This might include training for personal support assistants, planning accessible activities in an accessible environment, flexibility in terms of toilet arrangements and the provision of flexible transport. It might also include the individual education plans that you set for the children concerned (Chapter 5).

● Make sure that your admissions policy states that your setting does not discriminate against disabled pupils in the education, day care or other services it provides.

Disability and SEN

Many children who have disabilities will also have SEN (and vice-versa) but certainly not all. A child with a shortened limb may have learned to take part in all your early years activities without the need for any special adjustments. A child with a hearing impairment corrected by a hearing aid may be included in what you are doing without the need for anything additional or different. The diagram on the following page might be helpful in explaining the overlap.

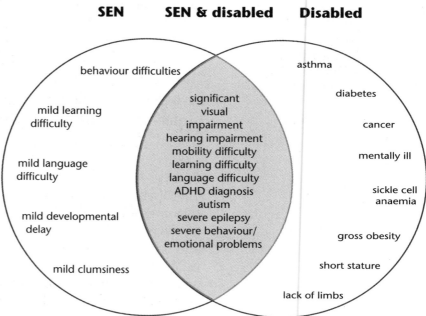

| | SEN | SEN & disabled | Disabled |

significant
visual
impairment
hearing impairment
mobility difficulty
learning difficulty
language difficulty
ADHD diagnosis
autism
severe epilepsy
severe behaviour/
emotional problems

behaviour difficulties

mild learning
difficulty

mild language
difficulty

mild developmental
delay

mild clumsiness

asthma

diabetes

cancer

mentally ill

sickle cell
anaemia

gross obesity

short stature

lack of limbs

© *Richard Rieser and Christine O'Mahoney, Disability Equality in Education, www.diseed.org.uk*

You will find the publication *Disability Equality in the Classroom: a human rights issue* by Richard Rieser and Micheline Mason extremely useful in planning your SEN policy and training staff. It is published by Disability Equality in Education (who also provide training): Unit GL, Leroy House, 436 Essex Road, London N1 3QP, www.diseed.org.uk.

What are reasonable adjustments?

The detail of the SEN Disability Act is still being tested in court and so the implications for settings will become clearer over the next few years. In the meantime, these examples would all be viewed as 'reasonable adjustments'.

● Make sure that your admissions policy does not state that all children have to be toilet-trained to attend. This would be seen as less favourable treatment for a child who has an impairing condition. All early years settings have to have arrangements to cope with 'accidents' and so you would be expected to make arrangements to change the child and dispose of soiled materials.

● Plan well ahead for any outings so that all children (even those with mobility problems) can come too. If necessary, choose a better venue, borrow a more appropriate buggy or arrange extra support.

● If you are short of staff on an outing, it would probably be seen as a reasonable adjustment to invite a parent or carer to come too in order to help.

● Make sure that children who cannot walk or stand are not left out – plan an alternative activity which is at floor level and includes all the children.

● Never exclude a child from choices just because of their impairing condition. For example, if you exclude a child from a sticking activity because that child has a learning difficulty and tends to eat the glue, this might be seen as less favourable treatment. Instead, plan for adult support and set up a reward system for not eating the glue.

● If you offer different options at snack time, make sure that all the children have choices, but limit them (for example) to gluten-free for those on a gluten-free diet.

● Start thinking about the physical access to your buildings. It might be possible to use a wooden ramp or an alternative entrance door for a child with a buggy or walking frame. If this is impossible, then the LEA should look for alternative provision outside the usual catchment area.

● You cannot deny a child from joining your setting because they are at an earlier developmental stage – instead, you should carry out an assessment and plan for their individual needs, following the SEN Code of Practice.

● Plan ways of including all the children in group time and circle time. If a child is non-verbal, look for alternative ways in which he or she can join in, answer the register and so on.

● Educate staff and parents/carers with clear information about HIV, AIDS and other conditions. Maintain confidential information on a need to know basis.

● Make individual behaviour plans for children whose behaviour is different in any way. Use risk-assessment to define those times and activities where extra supervision might be necessary in order to safeguard that child and the other children as well.

● Joint meetings with outside professional and with parents and carers would also be seen as useful steps towards planning your reasonable adjustments.

● Teach staff members some basic signs, and share these with all of the children.

● Always keep records which explain why you are making adjustments and how you are monitoring their effectiveness.

At the end of the day, making reasonable adjustments is common sense, so long as you have the right attitude towards inclusion. Try to see the session through the eyes of the child, make sure that all activities and spaces are accessible to that child and, if not, adjust what you are doing to fit. Keep a record of what you have done and why, and if you have any doubt, contact the Inclusion Officer in your local LEA Early Years Department.

Medical and social models of disability

We are in the middle of a revolution in terms of the way we view SEN and disability. It would be helpful if you shared with colleagues the distinction between a medical and a social model of disability so that they can begin to think more inclusively about the children. Traditionally, we have used a medical model in which the impairment of the child is seen as the problem. This leads to specialist assessment and diagnosis, special provision, special transport, early intervention, and words like 'management of the difficulty' or 'incurable'. In a social model, disabled people are seen as active fighters for equality working in partnership with allies. Here, the structures in society are seen as the problem. The issues can then be seen in a totally different light – lack of appropriate education, inaccessible buildings, discrimination in employment, segregated services, and lack of information. In early years, you have the flexibility and ethos to meet all needs inclusively and the next chapter focuses on how you can support colleagues in developing equal opportunities and anti-discriminatory practice for all children.

If you follow a social model of disability and SEN, these are the kinds of questions you will find yourself asking when you assess a child in your care:

- What are the child's strengths?
- What does the child enjoy?
- What help does the child need with dressing/undressing/going to the toilet/joining in and so on?
- How does the child let us know when he is she is happy/sad/cross/bored/anxious and so on?
- What help does the child need in each of the Areas of Learning and with the Foundation Stage curriculum as a whole?
- Will we need to make any changes to our physical access?
- What can we do to help the child learn and behave well?

CREATING EQUAL OPPORTUNITIES

Many SENCOs will be asked to take charge of equal opportunities in their setting. This chapter will help you to provide a welcoming environment for all the children you work with.

Understanding equal opportunities

It is often the SENCO who is asked to take the lead on equal opportunities in the setting, and a good starting point can be to make sure you have a totally inclusive SEN policy (Chapter 2). The Government's *Full Day Care National Standards* publication contains guidance on the standards that settings should aim for in all aspects of childcare including the provision of equal opportunities. Standard 9 states that a 'registered person' and staff should actively promote equality of opportunity and anti-discriminatory practice for all children. Often, this registered person is the SENCO.

To do this, the registered person should have, and periodically review, an equal opportunity policy which is consistent with current legislation and guidance. All children and adults should be treated with equal concern, and the registered person should have regard to relevant anti-discriminatory good practice. The registered person should also promote equal opportunities with regard to employment, training, admission to day care and access to the resources, activities and facilities available.

All staff and volunteers should understand and implement the equal opportunity policy. Parents and carers should have access to the equal opportunity policy. The registered person should liaise with parents/carers to ensure that all children's records contain information which enables the best care for their child. Look for ways of welcoming and accepting all children and their families, breaking down family isolation and building trusting relationships.

Anti-discriminatory practice

A setting whose practice is anti-discriminatory will:
● value and celebrate differences in identities, cultures, religions, abilities and social practices.
● recognise the impact of the social inequalities that exist in wider society and their effect on the lives of young children and their families.
● value children and adults for their individuality and ensure a sense of belonging that promotes self esteem. It will respect where children come from and what they bring to the learning situation.
● appreciate the importance of what is learned and unlearned in the early years.

If you are going to plan a curriculum of activities which is completely non-biased and accessible to all children, then you need

to develop positive attitudes about providing equal opportunities and these should pervade all that you think and do at work, at home and in society. It is one thing to make sure that your activities do not discriminate in any way by allowing one group of children to experience success more than another. It is far better to actually counter anything divisive through planning anti-discriminatory practice. You will be able to support colleagues better in this area if you can share an understanding of the issues which face families in relation to gender, ethnicity, sexuality, class and disability and the impact that discrimination can have on children's chances.

Article 2 of the United Nations Convention on the Rights of the Child in 1989 stated that every child has the right to live free from discrimination. The Full Day Care National Standards (DfES) make it clear that children need to feel valued and be free from discrimination. Now that many SENCOs are also being asked to be responsible for ensuring equal opportunities within their settings, what strategies can they use to make sure that staff adopt an anti-discriminatory way of working with the children?

● Help staff become aware of how sensitive young children can be. They soon pick up messages about who is 'better' or has more power than anyone else in the setting.

● Help staff assess what subtle messages might be expressed by their daily practice, the resources and the curriculum in your setting. Look at your books, toys, home corner and activities: do they represent a wide range of diversity and present positive images?

● Make sure that your admissions policy does not (unintentionally) exclude any group. For example, do you insist on children being toilet-trained and will this make sure that the very children who need you most cannot attend your setting?

● Help staff to develop non-judgmental language and respect for diversity. The baggage that staff bring from their own previous experiences and attitudes can colour the way they respond to different groups within the community. For example, they may stigmatise parents/carers of a disabled child as 'over-protective' if they already have firm views of what 'good parenting' is.

● Help staff see that treating children the same is not the same as treating them equally. They need to recognise that the world is not a level playing field and some children will need more help than others if they are to reach their entitlements as future members of the community.

Using dolls for children to identify with

What factors might contribute to a child becoming a target for discrimination? Other children might single them out for ridicule or exclude them in some way on account of the fact that:
● they dress differently
● they are physically different from the others (for example, through skin colour, weight or disability)
● they come from a minority cultural, ethnic or religious group
● they behave differently and that this is perceived as abnormal in some way
● they cannot speak the same language
● they find it hard to communicate with others (perhaps because of a sensory impairment or learning disability).

All children are gradually building up their self-identity and self-esteem in the early years and it is so important that they come to see themselves and their unique individuality as something positive and to be respected. One brilliant and utterly practical way of helping this (whether or not you have wide diversity represented in the community you serve) is through the use of persona dolls. These are dolls (and you can make or adapt your own) to which you give a persona such as a particular ethnicity, a disability or a certain way of life or religion.

A persona doll can be given any persona you wish in order to share information and develop values in the children. You could introduce 'Polly' to the children. Polly has a tiny hearing aid which you have crafted from moulded wax in her ear (use your creativity!). She loves to play in the sand, the water and especially out of doors. Tell a story about all the things Polly loves to do at nursery. At some point, one of the children will notice the tiny hearing aid. Explain that when Polly was a baby, her mum and dad found that she could not hear things clearly. She saw a special doctor and she was given a tiny hearing aid to make it easier for her to hear. However, she still has to look at you to hear you properly (role play this with Polly and the children). This can lead into a very natural conversation about Polly's needs and can serve as a useful introduction to a child with a hearing impairment joining the group or simply to widen children's understanding of different people's needs.

The important thing is that Polly does not join the general toy box. She has a place of honour on the shelf or desk where she can be reached for from time to time to share activities with the children (such as action rhymes with signing) or to make a particular point. Polly can have many friends. You might have Jamie in his wheelchair, Freya from a new-age travelling family, Tariq whose grandparents

came to this country from Egypt, Jed who lives with his aunt and uncle, Luke whose family attend worship at a church... all of whom can share the story of their daily lives. The variations are limitless and, with your own positive attitude and creativity, can fill any niche in your anti-discriminatory thinking. Through the use of persona dolls, children begin to identify with others who may be 'different' in some way, and through this can develop respect and understanding. It also gives you the chance to answer some of the awkward questions which children will sometimes ask in front of each other!

Gathering resources

As SENCO, it will be helpful if you can gather together resources and contacts which are going to help staff develop their anti-dicriminatory practice. Remember – this kind of practice is not just for settings who already cater for a wide range of children and diversity – it is for everyone. Here are some starting points.

● *Unlearning Discrimination in the Early Years* by Babette Brown (Trentham Books).
● *From Cradle to School: a practical guide to racial equality in early childhood education and care* is produced by the Commission for Racial Equality (0870 240 36 97).
● *Anti-Bias Curriculum: tools for empowering young children* by L. Derman-Sparks and the ABC Task Force (National Association for the Education of Young Children, Washington).
● Oxfam Education (020 7931 7660) provide resource packs, games, books and posters.
● Acorn Percussion (020 7720 2243) provide quality general and multicultural musical instruments.
● One World Book Company (020 7381 4994) supplies books from a black and multicultural perspective and picture books, many of which will appeal to boys.
● Community Insight (01793 512 612) stocks books for staff working with children on equal opportunities including special needs.
● Lillian Reeve (020 7221 2630) supplies hand-made mixed

parentage, Asian and Caribbean rag dolls.
● *Anti-bias approaches in the early years* is available from Save the Children (020 7700 8127).

CHILD-CENTRED ASSESSMENT AND IEPS

This chapter deals with how you can help your colleagues to identify, support and monitor SEN, and how practitioners can help children to get the most from their time in a setting.

What do we mean by SEN?

As SENCO, you are likely to find yourself in the position of 'gatekeeper' for which children's names are put on the setting's SEN register and which are not. Colleagues may be asking you to make a judgement on whether or not a child has special educational needs, and you may feel that you are not specialist enough to do this. In fact, it is the perceptions of your colleagues which are misplaced, and not your own specialism. In this chapter, we try to make the concept of 'special educational needs' a practical and workable one which colleagues can grasp more easily. An SEN is not something which resides within a child and must be spotted. It is simply a collection of needs which seem to require more than your usual range of approaches and support.

The idea from the SEN Code of Practice that children with SEN need something additional or different makes the whole issue much clearer. Turning this statement around, you can define special educational needs as those which appear to require more than your usual array of resources and support. As an early years setting, you will already be expected to be able to cater for a wide range of maturities, behaviours and stages. Therefore, there will not be a large number of children who seem to need even more than you are already providing. Nevertheless, there will be children who have disabilities and diagnosed conditions which you already know will require additional or different approaches. These children may have been assessed already by a local Child Development Centre or within the community. There will be others who, as you allow them to settle and get to know them better, will appear to need that extra attention and support as well. For these children, it will be you yourselves who are identifying and planning for the SEN through the Early Years Action and Early Years Action Plus which you are taking.

Children can have SEN for many different reasons and all of these are said to cause 'learning difficulties'. Sometimes you know the reasons – perhaps a child has grown up with a condition which affects their development such as Down's syndrome, or perhaps they are delayed in their ability to speak and communicate because of autism. Help colleagues to understand that these children do not have special needs because they look different, because they have a particular label or because they behave in an unusual way. They have special needs because they fail to make acceptable progress even when you have tried all your usual approaches. It is you, the early years practitioners and SENCO, who are experts in early years approaches and monitoring. Therefore you do not have to be an SEN specialist to identify and support SEN in the early years.

Early identification

The SEN Code of Practice gives you guidance on how to meet SEN in your setting. As a SENCO, you will already be familiar with this. There is fuller information in the *Special Needs Handbook* by Hannah Mortimer (Scholastic). Encourage staff to allow all children time to settle in and respond to the usual approaches for differentiating the early years curriculum before you assume they have SEN. Sometimes you will be able to help and advise at this early stage by offering general advice or showing staff how to differentiate the curriculum more effectively.

If staff members still feel concerned, you can help them by showing them how to gather information through observation and record keeping. That member of staff should be doing this for all the children anyway so the system for monitoring a child who has SEN can arise naturally from the existing approaches, but be in much more detail. Ask members of staff to use diary records, photographs, examples of the child's work and creations to build up a dossier of the child's interests, strengths, progress and areas of need. You might wish to collect checklists and observation schedules to aid what you are doing, and some groups have found it helpful to break the Stepping Stones down into even smaller steps for recording progress – for example as in the *3–5 Trackers* and the *Playladders* checklists by Hannah Mortimer (QEd).

Writing IEPs

Individual education plans should be a key feature of planning for any SEN in your group either as part of your Early Years Action or your Early Years Action Plus. They are also used regularly for children who have statements of SEN. As you will know, they should contain three or four short-term targets and make it clear how you will know that your teaching has been successful. They should lead to the child making progress and should be seen as an integrated aspect of the curriculum planning for the whole group. Bearing in mind our definition of SEN (above), they only include that which is additional to or different from the regular early years curriculum that is in place for all the children. There is no set format, and you need to design an

IEP which is clear, accessible and understandable for your setting. No-one ever prescribed that IEPs should be formal looking documents – why not use your IT skills and creativity to produce an IEP which looks child-centred and appealing to children and parents/carers? You will find an example on pages 50 and 51 which can be photocopied back-to-back. A less formal-looking document might also make it more likely that colleagues will see it through into action. You can also add sections which make sure that the child is actually consulted and involved in the IEP as well. Even if that child cannot speak, there will be opportunities for the child to show you through play and the expression of feelings what things are important to them and where they need you most. Try to record the nature of the child's difficulty in clear language rather than specialist labels and jargon.

You will find it easiest at first to sit down with colleagues to help them write 'SMART' targets – specific, measurable, achievable, realistic and time bound (for example 'by the end of this term, Beccy will be able to hold her pencil correctly and write her first name').

The temptation will always be for you to get on with writing it yourself, but this will make it harder to delegate the responsibility to other staff members later on. In the author's experience, IEPs are more likely to be followed through if the teacher actually involved with the child has written and monitored them. You will find a useful training exercise in Chapter 10. As you sit with the teacher to write the IEP, you can begin to discuss how that teacher will be able to differentiate the activities in order to make the curriculum accessible to those children who have SEN. Again, there are ideas for training in Chapter 10.

Monitoring IEPs

You may be feeling that it is one thing to assist colleagues in the writing of their IEPs but it is another thing altogether to make sure that they actually implement them effectively in their day-to-day planning! How can you support staff in the daily work they do to include children who have SEN?

● Provide general information about the range of needs and conditions staff members are likely to come across in their practice. You should find *The essential A–Z guide to special needs* by Hannah Mortimer (Scholastic) a useful reference for colleagues.

● Provide general training on target-setting, IEP planning and differentiation. You will find more ideas for this in Chapter 10.

● Build on staff's expertise by showing them how they can use the Foundation Stage curriculum and Stepping Stones to map a child's development at present and plan next steps and targets.

● If a child's development is very delayed, you might need to 'track back' further, perhaps making reference to the P Scales, designed for older children whose development is severely delayed (*Supporting the target setting process: Guidance for effective target setting for pupils with SEN*, QCA/DfES). You can also make use of developmental checklists such as the checklist from the *Portage Early Education Programme* (nferNelson) or the *0–3 Trackers* (QEd).

● Invest a little time in showing staff members how their individual planning for one child can fit into the planning of activities for all the children. They might need your help to see that special support is not the same as one-to-one, but that they can actually support children inclusively in the group.

● Offer regular consultation (page 52) or 'SENCO clinics' for staff members to report back briefly on how their target setting and monitoring is going and to offer further advice on differentiation. You do not need to know all the answers – simply where to look for them or who to ask.

● Build on staff members' creativity in designing ways of involving the children in their planning through offering them choices, listening to them speak, interpreting their play and reactions and getting to know the child thoroughly as an individual.

● Meet with the staff member prior to the IEP review meeting (Chapter 6) and help them prepare the progress report. Refer to the Foundation Stage curriculum together and decide in which Areas of Learning you would ideally like to see the next targets being set. Talk about ways of consulting the child/involving the child in the review. Even if you feel that the child should not be present, photographic records, especially if a child has control of the camera, can be extremely useful.

● Provide support and encouragement to staff members working with SEN and make sure you receive support as well, perhaps from your manager, Area SENCO or an outside support professional.

ARRANGING MEETINGS AND REVIEWS

This chapter deals with organising and conducting meetings and reviews for parents, carers and all the people involved in educating a child with SEN or other disabilities.

How to arrange reviews

As SENCO, you will need to call regular review meetings for any child whose needs are being monitored through Early Years Action or Early Years Action Plus. Sometimes in larger settings, it is the teacher most involved with the child who calls this meeting, with the SENCO's guidance and support. Here are some pointers for arranging these review meetings.

● Aim for review meetings at least once a term.

● If there are many children's names on the SEN register, try to stagger the reviews so that they are evenly spaced (there is a possible format to record dates on page 53).

● Set the date at least a month ahead and if possible, set a date for the next review when you are all together at the previous one.

● Choose an accessible but quiet place to meet – perhaps in the playroom at the end of the session with refreshments and comfortable chairs.

● Consider family needs, such as the need for a translator, the need for a créche facility, or the need for disabled access.

● Write to parents, carers and everyone directly involved with the child's IEP (even if you have met people in passing or set the date a term earlier) – you will find a possible format on page 54.

● Decide which other professionals need to be involved. A support teacher or speech and language therapist directly involved in advising you on the child's progress should certainly be invited to come or to send a report. A paediatrician or specialist seeing the child for occasional reviews might not be able to come, but the

health visitor or school doctor might be able to provide you with a link to any relevant medical information. If the child is about to transfer to another setting or school, invite the receiving teacher, practitioner or SENCO to join you. Finally, ask parents or carers if there are any other professionals or parental supporters who they would like to be present.

● Gather information about progress across the six Areas of Learning. It is always best if the teacher or adult most closely involved can be present at the review so that they can provide a verbal report as well.

● Find a way of helping parents or carers prepare for the meeting. There is a photocopiable proforma which you should find helpful on page 55.

● If a child has a statement of SEN, the LEA should tell you when to call reviews and should provide a form for recording the meeting. Usually these statement reviews are six-monthly in the early years. You can still use the format on page 53 to keep tabs on when they are expected and to chase them up with the LEA if necessary.

The review meeting

The most effective review meetings are those which feel both professional and informal. As SENCO, you are likely to be chairing this meeting (rather than any visiting professional). Try to make everyone feel welcome and confident enough to say what they need to say – you are already highly skilled in doing this with children! Sit in a circle and start by going round the group introducing who you are and explaining how you are involved with the child. For example 'My name is Mary. I am the SENCO, which means that I co-ordinate all the support for any child who seems to need something a bit different or extra than usual. It is my job to chair this meeting and to make sure we are helping and including _child's name_ in the best way we possibly can'.

Remember that parents and carers are the experts on their own children, but it is your expertise in asking the right questions which will yield the information you need to work in partnership with them. You may decide that it is fine to have other young members of the family present, but be aware of the need to share the load so that parents and carers can be involved in the meeting as well as looking after their children.

Find a format to record the review meeting which suits your situation. You will find a photocopiable example on page 56. Basically, you need to record who was present and who sent reports. Start with the positives and describe the progress that the child has made since the last review, listing the additional and extra support that you have put into place. Next, describe how helpful this support has been – this also gives you an opportunity to list any concerns anyone might still have. It is helpful at this point to mention any recent changes in the child's situation at home or in the setting that might have influenced progress – a recent hospital visit perhaps, or a family breakdown. Refer back to the targets of the previous review and note whether the targets on the previous IEP have been achieved. This leads you into negotiating the current IEP.

Finally, set the date of next review meeting and discuss to whom the present review report needs to be circulated. Some of you might decide to have a separate section on the views of parent and carers. Others might weave these seamlessly and inclusively into the whole document so that it represents all your views.

Running the meeting

Sometimes meetings do not go as smoothly as you would have liked. You can usually tell which meetings are likely to be problematic and prepare for them better by making time to talk things through beforehand. If you have found out why a parent or carer might be feeling defensive and have already taken steps to provide clearer information or to air certain issues, then the meeting should flow smoothly and serve to rubber stamp the ground you have already covered.

If discussions become heated, do your best to stay calm and impartial. Keep your voice level, firm and respectful and give time for each person to voice their views. There should be no excuse for a member of staff to become heated, so it may be a parent or carer who becomes emotional. If it is helpful, make detailed notes and keep reading them back to make sure that you are recording them correctly – this shows respect, yet slows the outburst down. If there are differing views, then these should be recorded as such (for example, 'Mrs Dodds did not agree with this and felt that...' or 'Sue felt that Darren's behaviour had improved a lot in the setting and Jim felt that there were still serious difficulties with his son's poor concentration' – the use of the word *and* instead of *but* can be a powerful tool in keeping the discussion going smoothly).

If one person is quiet throughout the review, make sure that they are brought into the discussion by asking them what they think or asking a question. Work with staff to help them ask positive open-ended questions: 'How much help does Tom need when he goes to the toilet?' is much less threatening than ' Is Tom toilet-trained yet?' Finally, make sure that the child is represented in some way – either by examples of work, photographs or video tape, or by having the

child present. Make a point of talking about what the child likes, what his or her strengths are, and where she or he would like most help. Make a definite end to the meeting by thanking everyone for coming, checking that everything has been covered and then standing up!

Writing summaries and reports

After the review meeting, write down the findings using your standard format, attaching any extra notes, reports and a copy of the IEP. As you become more practised, you will find you can do this as the meeting is in progress. There is usually no need to type this up so long as it is neat and clear, though some settings prefer the review record to be word-processed so that it looks more formal. Copy it to all those who attended the review meeting, to parents and carers, and to outside professionals who attended the meeting, sent reports or who are about to become involved.

Sometimes, a parent or carer will not attend the meeting. Send a follow-up letter to them along these lines:

> I am sorry you were unable to come to the meeting about _____'s progress on _____. In view of his/her difficulties, it has been decided that we should take Early Years Action/Plus. This means that we will be planning extra support to help progress in the future. I enclose a copy of the individual education plan that we agreed at the meeting so that you can see what we are planning. It would be helpful if you could call in so that we can discuss this together on _____. Our next review meeting will be on _____, and I also enclose a copy of our special needs policy to provide you with more information about the support we can offer. Yours sincerely _____

Occasionally, you might find yourself asked to send a written report to an outside professional who is working with the child. You will find it easiest if you follow a set format and stick to the information you already know. You might send a copy of the most recent progress report or review meeting, or summarise the progress the child has made on the six Areas of Learning. It is good practice to let parents and carers know that you are doing this. Add a covering letter with any particular observations which you think might be helpful – how well the child settled, what seems to work best, what are your greatest concerns and where you feel you need help and advice.

WORKING WITH FAMILIES

Chapter seven is about the sensitive issue of how you can establish positive relationships with parents, carers and families as they come to terms with the fact that their child has SEN or other disabilities.

Parent Partnership

The involvement of parents and carers at all stages is a basic principle of the SEN Code of Practice.

The basic principles of Parent Partnership and how to develop it effectively are covered in another book from this series, *Special Needs Handbook* by Hannah Mortimer (Scholastic).

In this chapter, there are some ideas for helping you communicate effectively with parents and carers in your role as SENCO. In particular, you can help in these areas:

● Supporting colleagues in their need to acknowledge the fundamental role that parents and carers have already played in their child's education and help them gather information before the child joins the setting.

● Looking for ways of helping colleagues share the responsibility for learning between home and setting. This is done through mutual respect, ongoing communication and regular information.

● Making sure that parents and carers of children who are experiencing SEN feel welcome in your setting and that there are opportunities for calling in or keeping in touch regularly.

● Acting as a mediator or troubleshooter when difficulties in communicating or sharing information arise.

Feelings and stresses

When a child first starts in a new setting, it is a sensitive time for all parents and carers. Add to this the particular concerns and mixed emotions which parents and carers of a child with SEN might have, and you can understand that sensitive handling will be vital for effective partnership with parents/carers. When parents or carers are first told that their child might be disabled or have special needs, they can experience a whole range of overwhelming emotions.

There are often feelings of inadequacy, bereavement, anger and grief. To this can be added denial and helplessness. It helps if you can try to tune in to some of these emotional reactions which you might be picking up from a parent/carer. There may be feelings of guilt ('What did we do wrong?'). There may be a tendency to blame each other or the setting. They may not trust you to cope. They may be hanging on your every word in case they feel that you are rejecting their child. Try to understand all of this if, at first, a parent or carer seems defensive or 'prickly' towards you.

Tuning In

What can you do to become as sensitive as possible to parents'/carers' feelings and emotions?

● Try to understand why parents/carers might be saying something. What does this tell you about the way they are feeling? One way to do this is to think about how they are making you feel at that point in time. If they make you feel angry, they are probably angry themselves and you need to defuse the situation by not adding to the confrontation until things are calmer. If they make you feel sad, they may be depressed and need your nurturing and understanding. If you are left confused, then they are probably feeling very muddled themselves and need your clear information and guidance. If they are making you feel anxious, then that is probably just what they are feeling themselves.

● Share clear information about your early years curriculum in order to inform parents and carers about what you hope to achieve for their child at each age and stage. It is helpful if parents and carers are involved in the early years sessions wherever possible so they can see what you are trying to achieve, particularly for those children who have SEN.

● Helpless or troubled parents and carers need practical workable advice, but they don't need to feel that the professionals are the successful ones and they, the carers, are failing. Carers with low self-esteem and high stress are quick to pick up the fact that they are 'not doing it right'. This leads to resentfulness and avoidance.

● Instead, home–school activities should be negotiated and encouraging and warm suggestions given. 'What seems to keep his attention at home?' 'What toys would be good for teaching this activity?' 'What help do you need from us?'

● Encourage colleagues to use regular play plans which contain activities for a child and carer to do at home to support the work you are doing in the setting. You will find an example on page 57.

● If a parent/carer denies there is anything wrong, start with where carers are at in terms of their understanding, but make it clear what

might happen next. Once any plan has been agreed, you should be firm, stick to your plan, and continue to involve parents and carers with every sign of progress or need, making it clear that you are doing this in order to keep them in touch.

● If a parent/carer cannot or will not stop to talk, negotiate a home visit to meet on their home territory. Start by finding out what their views and feelings are; this gives important information to you about how you can introduce your own concerns.

● Do not be tempted to see parents/carers as over anxious. Their views should always be taken seriously, and point by point reassurance can be given with concrete evidence that all is well.

● Sometimes, parents/carers might realise there is a problem, but refuse any kind of outside help, even though the providers are convinced that things have come to that stage. Explain how it is you that need the outside advice and support in order to provide the best help for their child. Perhaps agree to do your best without outside help at one review meeting, but agree in advance that you will need to refer the child to an outside professional at the next review meeting if the targets have not been met. Explain that this is because you yourselves will need further advice – this avoids the suggestion that there is something wrong with their child.

Asking questions

Invest time gathering information and establishing a relationship with child and parents/carers before the child joins your setting. A home visit is usually helpful, sharing photographs of your group and talking about your typical sessions. Asking positive, open-ended questions can provide information about the child's strengths and about the kind of help that they need. Parents/carers soon feel discouraged if they find themselves listing all the things their child cannot do. Take time to ask parents or carers what they would like the setting to do to help, taking care they are not left feeling that they have failed in some way. Taking trouble to share the good news from the start helps any bad news to fall more into context. Above all, SENCOs can show that they care and that they are trying to work alongside parents/carers to help the child. You will find a group exercise for encouraging colleagues to frame their questions to parents/carers in a positive way on page 62.

When feelings become strong

From time to time, you may find yourself having to deal with an angry or tearful outburst from a parent or a carer. During an episode of extreme anger, the body becomes flooded with adrenaline. This is a primitive biological reaction which happens to every one of us and which is geared to putting the mind and body on the alert for either fight or flight. The brain becomes hyper-aroused and every sense is alert to what is going on. The person stops thinking clearly and reacts emotionally. The adrenaline remains high for many minutes afterwards as the body readies itself for further trouble. After a while, the physiological state returns to normal and that person calms down. Some people liken this reaction to a spark igniting a fuse, the fuse burning for a while and then the firework exploding. The point is that you cannot put out the firework once the fuse has been lit, though you can identify when this happens, and you can wait until the firework has lost its power before intervening. This approach is called 'anger management'.

In very simple terms, when people to whom you are speaking become stressed or angry, they are using their emotional brains more than their logical brains. They may find themselves doing or saying things which they later regret. When a parent or carer becomes very upset, there is no point in appealing to logic – they first have to calm down if they are to be in a position where they can take in information and handle it in a logical and reasoned way. There are certain basic approaches for ensuring your own safety and avoiding making the situation worse.

● If faced with anger, give respectful eye contact but stand diagonally so that you are not face-on and not glaring.
● Keep a distance between you that is over an arm's length. Make sure that the exit is clear to you if you have to move away quickly.
● Present an outward demeanour of calmness (however you feel inside). Watch your voice especially and try to keep this calm and level.
● Make yourself less threatening by not challenging their statements at this stage.
● If faced with distress, move away from any audience and speak calmly and reassuringly to parents/carers until their feelings subside.
● Listen and use statements that affirm the way the other person is feeling. For example, 'I see that you are very upset about this', 'What a shame this had to happen to you', 'I hear what you say'.

● Let the feelings run their course and watch for them to die down. Then change the situation altogether by suggesting that you need to talk about this and to see how you can help.
● Move to a calm area away from an audience, offer parents or carers a warm drink and begin to engage their logical brains again by talking rationally about how you can move things forward.

WORKING WITH OTHER PROFESSIONALS

This chapter discusses the fact that the SENCO is part of a large team of professionals who must work together co-operatively in order to best support the child.

Who else can help?

As part of the SENCO role, you need to collect information and details for all the professionals and services which might be able to support you. First of all, you should find out who your contact might be in each area, what sort of help they can offer you, at what level of concern you can contact them, and how you can access their services.

Clinical Child Psychologists:
- offer family support, counselling and often family or play therapy
- help with attachment difficulties between carers and children
- provide cognitive and developmental assessment where there are concerns
- give advice on behaviour management and specialist conditions such as autism
- can be contacted via the health visitor or GP.

Community Doctors and Paediatricians:
- can identify cause and diagnosis of a medical condition
- can arrange for parents and families to receive genetic counselling
- can monitor hearing and vision
- provide medical input to the statutory assessment of SEN
- can be contacted via the health visitor or GP.

Early Years Support Teachers:
- can give you general advice on your Early Years Action and may be directly involved with a child as part of Early Years Action Plus
- might provide educational advice as part of a statutory assessment of SEN
- can be contacted through the LEA or Sure Start Partnership.

Educational Psychologists:
- help parents, carers and those who work in settings to find solutions to children's difficulties or individual needs
- can give you general help to clarify and define the problem, generate teaching and management approaches and evaluate the success of these
- can provide specialist assessment of all kinds of learning difficulties.
- always become involved if a child is being statutorily assessed
- can be contacted via the LEA support services by making a referral at Early Years Action Plus.

Occupational Therapists:
- aim to develop the child's maximum level of independence in life and improve self-help skills
- assess gross and fine motor skills, including dyspraxic difficulties, writing, independence skills, coping skills, visual perception and body awareness
- assess the need for specialised equipment for home and pre-school including seating, wheelchairs, toilet and bathing aids, adaptive equipment to improve everyday skills
- advise settings about the proper use of special equipment, aids and apparatus
- are usually contacted via the Child Development Centre or the health visitor.

Physiotherapists:
- work towards helping the child reach his or her maximum potential in movement and balance
- provide advice on positioning and movement for children with physical disabilities
- provide direct physiotherapy for children or design programmes of exercise for other people to use with the children who need it
- are usually involved as part of a Child Development service or hospital service.

Portage Workers:
- undertake regular home visits to assess where a child has reached in each area of development, to negotiate what to teach next, and to model how to teach it
- usually become involved if a child's development is at least a year behind in any area
- are often based in local Portage services accessed via the Child Development Centre or Early Years Support Service.

Social Workers:
- provide counselling and support to vulnerable or stressed families
- have access to Social Services provision, including day nurseries, respite care, shared caring, and early years support schemes
- play a crucial and statutory role in child protection procedures
- can provide general advice on whether or not you should take action on child protection
- can be contacted via their customer service department at the local Social Services offices.

Speech and Language Therapists:
- offer assessment, treatment, and advice on speech, language and communication development
- advise on feeding and swallowing problems
- provide training and advice on signing and alternative methods of communicating
- can be contacted via the health visitor, GP and sometimes the LEA support service.

Confidentiality

Working with outside professionals can sometimes raise tricky issues of confidentiality. Here are some pointers.

● The information from health professionals will be confidential so do not be surprised if it cannot be sent directly to you.

● The best practice is to access any reports through parents and carers. Otherwise, if this proves problematic, contact the local school nurse or community doctor for advice.

● Never copy other professionals' reports without permission.

● Keep all confidential reports in a locked cabinet and operate a need to know policy for sharing sensitive information.

● Never promise absolute confidentiality to a child or carer. You need to make it clear that your involvement cannot be confidential if you see the need to protect the child or report criminal activity.

Joint planning

When a child with a disability or SEN transfers into your early years setting, it can be invaluable to hold a planning meeting in order to help people think through the needs of individual children and how these might be met in the setting. Do not wait to be invited to one; set this up yourself if you feel it would be helpful. The Early Years Support Teacher should be able to give you advice. You will find it best to contact professionals well ahead, asking:

(a) if they feel it would be useful to come

(b) if not, would they would contribute a report?

(c) and suitable times.

You can then find a date that suits most of you, making sure that it also suits parents or carers.

The purpose of the initial joint planning meeting would be:

● gathering and sharing all the information you are going to need to help the child

● planning the start

● planning your approaches and how they will be monitored

● handing over between professionals

● establishing good communications

● establishing positive relationships

● reassuring parents and carers

● reassuring and supporting any staff who will be in direct contact with the child

● addressing potential difficulties early on

● detailing the need for any special resources from outside your school or nursery.

There is a photocopiable proforma to use or adapt on page 58.

Working as a consultant

One way in which the SENCO can help staff develop confidence and skills in working with SEN is to use a consultative approach. This approach is often used by outside professionals working with the setting but it can also be adapted for SENCOs to use with staff. A consultation is an exploration of a difficulty or concern and in this example, that concern is about a child's level of language ability. You

might decide to hold a regular slot each week in which the SENCO meets with staff to explore any concerns or interventions to be tried with the children who have SEN. The aim is for you to explore a concern and reach a better understanding of what is going on using joint problem solving. This should help you all to work out more effective approaches and strategies.

Planning an SEN consultation

● Agree a time limit to discuss each child.

● Find a quiet area where you will not be disturbed and can switch off your mobile phones.

● Make sure that you have arranged a time when those members of staff who know the child best will be present.

● Use the photocopiable format on page 52 to direct the discussion.

● Help staff put into words what it is they are concerned about and why. It helps if you can encourage them to find clear unambiguous words to do this, for example 'I have only heard Sanjay use two words together and I want to help him speak in fuller phrases'.

● Then encourage the staff to talk about what approaches they have tried so far. For example, 'I tried sitting down with him and talking about photographs from home. Sanjay tended to point rather than to speak. I wonder how much he understands?' The very fact that you are meeting regularly in this way encourages staff to see SEN not just as a something to be identified and labelled, but an area of need to be worked on.

● Ask them what effects they have noticed following their interventions. For example, staff might notice that Sanjay seems to look and listen better when he is in a small group and he is at his most vocal when playing with the water. It will be helpful here to have the voices of different members of staff who might have seen the situation differently or have tried different approaches with differing success. Again, the fact that SEN consultation is a regular part of the SENCO support will make the whole experience one of staff sharing their different approaches rather than feeling threatened or intimidated.

● Ask staff what progress they would like to see following their interventions. For example, 'Sanjay will be happy to talk to a familiar adult about something he is interested in, using short phrases in his first language'. Begin to talk about how this might be done, building on the staff's own ideas and your own knowledge of good practice.

● Explore whether there are any other factors that you think might be important.

● Talk about how parents or carers are involved in their child's SEN and what they feel about progress.

● Make a note of any other agency involved and what their input has been or might be in the future.

● Make sure that you end up with clear conclusions, strategies and actions and that everyone understands what these are.

● Keep a record of the discussion – this may become part of your 'evidence' for monitoring any SEN in the future.

Meet up again in three weeks to review progress and decide on 'next steps'.

SPECIAL NEEDS **in the early years**: SEN Co-ordinator's handbook

POSITIVE APPROACHES FOR DIFFICULT PROBLEMS

This chapter deals with how your setting decides that a behaviour has become a problem, and what is the best approach for everyone to take in this situation.

Supporting colleagues

Each SENCO has a responsibility to pass on information about behaviour management to staff members through training and ongoing support. In this chapter, you will think about how you can help staff members decide when a behaviour becomes a problem, gather information about that problem and plan an intervention for changing it. If staff talk to you about 'a problem child', it can be useful to sit down with them and help them redefine the problem as a 'problem behaviour' rather than something which is within the child. That way, staff can be helped to see that there is something they can actually do to encourage more appropriate behaviour.

Observation and assessment

The first step with a behaviour difficulty is to help colleagues gather information through talking with the family, any other professional involved and through observing the behaviour itself. Not only does this provide you with useful information but it gives you thinking time to work out what you can do about it. Once a problem has been identified, everyone will be looking towards you to do something. When you gather information, you are clearly doing something even though you may not have a plan of action formulated. Sometimes, the very act of standing back a little and observing what is going on gives you and your colleagues the emotional distance to think about the problem more objectively and come to a more informed decision about your course of action.

Gathering information

There are several methods which you can suggest to staff for gathering information about a difficult behaviour.

ABC Diary

Ask staff to keep a diary recording what the child was actually doing, what seemed to lead up to it and what the consequences were. Encourage them to write clearly and objectively, describing observable actions and using non-judgemental language. This is called an 'ABC' diary because it records:

A – the antecedent – what led up to the behaviour or what was happening just before it.

B – the behaviour itself in clear unambiguous words.

Encourage staff to use words like 'hit', 'threw', 'screamed' rather than 'was aggressive' 'was disruptive', 'was naughty'.

C – the consequences of the behaviour – what happened as a result.

Counting or measuring the behaviour

Sometimes a behaviour is so evident that you can actually count the number of times it happens during a session. Other behaviours can be measured in terms of their duration – perhaps a child screamed for ten minutes today or played happily for twenty minutes.

Spot observations

There are occasions when this can be a very helpful approach, depending on the behaviour being observed. For example, you could ask a staff member to collect spot observations. Supposing that staff were worried about a child whose behaviour was very solitary. Each five minutes one of them could observe the child briefly and record whether they were playing on their own or with others.

Behaviour charts

An 'ABC chart' can help to identify any factors that may be affecting the child's behaviour. Like the ABC diary, it allows you to gather information about all kinds of behaviour and not to identify the problem behaviour in advance. Ask the staff to record three or four significant incidents of 'difficult' behaviour on a chart such as this.

ABC behaviour chart			
Time	Behaviour	What led up to it?	What happened next?

For every entry of a difficult behaviour, staff should be asked to record one occasion when the child was behaving appropriately or well. This provides you with information about the situations which work well for the child as well as those which are less successful.

Fly on the wall observation

Ask a member of staff to observe a child over a continuous period of time (say 30 minutes) and to write down in clear, unambiguous terms, what they are doing and how they are interacting. Ask them to record the time in the left-hand margin so that you will have an idea of how long the child was playing in a certain area, with certain other children or demonstrating a certain behaviour. Arrange for extra help so that the observer can be released. Ask other staff to carry on as if the observer were not present and not to rely on that person to manage any incidents or help. Suggest that the observer sits somewhere to the side of the room and moves discreetly between areas to keep the child in view. Later, you can look through the observation together and identify any patterns to the behaviour.

Problem solving

● Once you have gathered as much information as you can about the child's behaviour, help staff select just one behaviour to work on first.

● Work with staff to decide on a hypothesis – what do you all think is keeping that behaviour going?

● Then draw up a plan together to change the antecedents, the behaviour or the consequences (see below).

● Monitor progress over three weeks and then review your hypothesis and your interventions if you need to. Behavioural approaches take a little while to work because they often lead to a child testing the new boundaries for a while.

Planning changes

What are the most common approaches you can advise staff to follow for changing the **antecedents** to a difficult behaviour?

● Avoid difficult situations by side-stepping/planning around them.

● Distract the child and reduce the number of confrontations.

● Make sure the activity or the expectations suits the child's level.

● Encourage staff to use the child's name and gain full attention before giving directions.

● Ask staff to give more positive attention before trouble happens.

● Suggest that they give the child a warning if they are going to change activity.

● Help them to anticipate problem times and be a step ahead.

● Encourage them to give clear directions and tell children what they should do as well as what they should not.

● Ask them to show the child what to do as well as saying it.

● Choose a few simple rules together and stick to them.

You can also help staff plan interventions that directly affect the child's **behaviour**.

● Stop the behaviour if they can safely and appropriately do so.

● Teach the child a new behaviour opposite to the first.

● Praise another behaviour incompatible with the first.

The third option is to plan interventions which change the **consequences** of a child's behaviour, making less likely to occur in the future.

● Help all staff to be absolutely consistent in managing behaviour.

● Reward when the child is not doing the inappropriate behaviour.

● Ask them to ignore attention-seeking behaviour whenever it is safe to do so.

● Help them make it more fun for the child to behave appropriately.

● Star charts and stickers can also work well. Staff should never remove one once given. There is an example of a sticker chart on page 59 which you can photocopy.

Managing stress

Having to work with very challenging behaviours is one of the most stressful things you and your colleagues will have to face. There are methods that can be used to reduce a stress reaction if staff can be helped to recognise what is causing it and how their body and brain are responding. This is called 'stress management' and these ideas

POSITIVE APPROACHES FOR DIFFICULT PROBLEMS

will be useful for sharing with staff members:
● Have a work-free zone somewhere in the setting where staff can relax when necessary – even if it is an armchair in a quiet corner!
● If a staff member is feeling extremely stressed, try to arrange relief so that they can take a five minute breather outside.
● Use careful planning to make sure that staff know what to do in certain difficult situations, for example when a child has a big temper tantrum.
● Hold regular relaxed get-togethers after difficult sessions to debrief and unwind.
● Encourage staff not to compare themselves with others, but to compare themselves with themselves. So what if they handled something not as they would have wished one day – this will help them do it better the next.
● Remind staff that nobody has to be perfect – just professional and good enough.
● Develop an ethos in which staff feel that it is OK to ask for help and support.

Staying positive

It sometimes comes as a surprise to newly qualified or inexperienced staff that we should be using positive approaches to dealing with what might appear to be very negative behaviours. Positive behavioural approaches do these things:
● They make sure that the child's self esteem remains positive. This is because the child is given the message that it is the behaviour which is unacceptable rather than the child.
● They are based on the use or removal of rewards and pleasant happenings. Negative consequences may work in the short-term to control or stop a difficult behaviour but they will not help the child to change behaviour in the longer term. Instead, they lead to children behaving inappropriately until an adult intervenes, rather than learning self control.
● They aim not only to remove or alter an inappropriate behaviour but to replace it with a more positive and appropriate behaviour. Since you are all in the business of delivering the Foundation Stage curriculum for Personal, social and emotional development, this makes obvious sense. You know that children do not arrive in your setting with good behaviour ready packaged. Behaviour and social skills need to be learned and developed just like everything else.

Further Reading

You will find that the book *Managing Children's Behaviour* by Dr Hannah Mortimer from Scholastic's *Early Years Training and Management* series goes into this approach in more detail, discussing what constitutes problem behaviour, explaining what practitioners can do to overcome it, and providing some useful training ideas.

ARRANGING A TRAINING EVENT

It is the SENCO's responsibility to design and conduct SEN training for colleagues. This chapter details a number of different activities which you can use to start implementing your training programme.

How we learn

When you are designing SEN training for your early years colleagues, it is important to consider how adults learn and what factors contribute not only to their learning new skills and acquiring new knowledge and beliefs, but to their putting these into practice in the longer term.

● First, adults must want to learn and will only learn effectively if they see the need for it. Make sure that your SEN training is valued within the setting and is seen as part of the regular continuing professional development (CPD).

● Adults learn best by doing. They can learn by listening and watching, but they are more likely to learn effectively if they actively do something. Your training needs to be full of practical examples and relevant activities.

● They will resist or reject new learning which does not fit easily with what they know already from experience. You have no choice but to start your training at the level of the participants, even if this is very basic indeed.

● Adults learn best in an informal environment. Make sure that everyone is comfortable and nurtured with refreshments. Create an ethos that makes each person feel confident and able to contribute.

● Adults need guidance not grading. They need feedback to tell them how well they are doing, but they fear other people knowing if they are doing badly. Develop the skills of using 'and' statements instead of but statements: 'I liked the way you decided to use the water play with this child and it would have been even more effective if you had involved another child to model ways of playing and sharing together'.

● The training material needs to be meaningful. The more meaningful to the trainee, the better the learning and the less people forget over time. You will find some possible handouts for your training which should fit in with what you already do in your setting in the photocopiables at the back of this book.

● Adults need regular practice in the new skills they are learning or new skills will disappear over time. They show relatively better recall of knowledge and skills if they have to apply them regularly. Plan follow-up to your training so that you can observe and support colleagues in practical situations.

● Adults achieve better performance if allowed to work at their own pace because of the learning styles and approaches that they will have developed over a number of years. Some of us learn best through looking, others through listening and others still through

doing. Plan training events which involve listening, observing, practicals and handouts.

Training activities

On the next three pages, you will find a selection of short training activities to start you off.

We believe ...

Encourage staff to take part in designing or reviewing the setting's SEN policy

Time
About one hour

What you need
- Photocopies of pages 49 and 63 (the evaluation form).
- Photocopies of your existing SEN policy if you are in the process of reviewing it.
- A flipchart and pens.

Preparation
- Read through Chapter 2.
- Write up 'What the policy should contain' (page 14) on one sheet.

What you do
- Hand out the copies of page 49 and your existing policy if available, one for each member of staff.
- Explain that you are going to write/review your SEN policy together and check that it is up-to-date.
- Ask your colleagues to work in pairs or small groups.
- Write up the wording you choose on a flipchart. Keep it simple and clear.
- Use the checklist on page 14 as a prompt to make sure your policy is inclusive.
- Agree to write up the policy and present it as a draft to parents, carers and management.
- Circulate the evaluation form and ask colleagues to complete it.

Smartly does it

Help staff members write clear and effective IEP targets.

Time
About one hour

What you need
- Photocopies of pages 50–51 and 63 (the evaluation form).
- The SEN Toolkit, Section 5 (see page 64)
- An overhead projector and acetates or a flipchart and pens
- Photocopies of real IEPs with personal details removed for confidentiality.

Preparation
- Photocopy the overheads on pages 1 to 4 of the SEN Toolkit Section 5 onto acetates or write the contents onto flipchart sheets.
- Read Chapter 5.

SPECIAL NEEDS **in the early years**: SEN Co-ordinator's handbook

What you do
● Go through the overheads from the SEN Toolkit which describe the management of individual education plans. Make them more practical by adding your own comments and examples.
● Hand out copies of pages 50–51 and the examples of IEPs.
● Write this on a sheet of paper or acetate as you talk through it:
SMART targets: Specific, Measurable, Achievable, Relevant and Time bound.
● Ask colleagues to work in pairs to discuss a child known to both of them and design 4 SMART targets for that child.
● Move around the pairs and support them as they work.
● Circulate the evaluation form and ask colleagues to complete it.

Eating dinosaurs

Help staff members understand the principles of differentiation.

Time
About 45 minutes

What you need
Photocopies of pages 60, 61 and 63 (the evaluation form).
A flipchart and pens

Preparation
● Write 'How do you eat a dinosaur? In small chunks!' on the flipchart

What you do
● Pass a copy of page 60 to each colleague.
● Go through the main ways of differentiating play and invite colleagues to think of any more.
● Divide colleagues into groups of three or four.
● Invite each group to think of a child known to them all and an activity that the child finds particularly difficult.
● Ask them to write down their ideas for differentiating that activity for that particular child.
● Ask them to think of further examples if there is time.
● Meet together to share their ideas.
● Give out copies of page 61 and show how it can be used to break activities down into smaller steps.
● Ask colleagues to put their ideas into action over the next week or two and plan together how this can be done.
● Circulate the evaluation form and ask colleagues to complete it.

Choosing the right words

Help staff members develop positive language for talking to parents or carers about SEN.

Time
About 45 minutes

What you need
Photocopies of pages 62 and 63 (the evaluation form).
A flipchart and pens

Preparation
Divide the first sheet into two columns. Write in the left-side of page 62 in the left column and leave a space on the right.

What you do
● Give out a copy of page 62 to each colleague.
● Explain that there are ways in which we can say just what we want to but in a positive way which does not threaten or upset anyone.
● Go through the first three as examples.
● Complete the right-hand-side of the rest of the page, working as a plenary group.
● Now divide colleagues into two teams. Each team sets a difficult question or statement for the second team to reword positively for a parent or carer.
● Complete several examples if there is time.
● Circulate the evaluation form and ask colleagues to complete it.

Setting play plans

Help staff members plan activities to share with parents and carers at home.

Time
About one hour

What you need
● Photocopies of pages 57 and 63 (the evaluation form).
● Photocopies of real IEPs with personal details removed for confidentiality.
● A flipchart and pens.
● Your usual range of toys, resources and equipment.

What you do
● Give out the copy of page 57 and go through it.
● Explain how play plans can be used to share activities between home and setting and to work closely with parents and carers.
● Think of a child you all know, decide on an area to work on and then design a play plan all together, writing it up on a sheet of flipchart.
● Now divide colleagues into groups of three or four. Give each group a copy of an IEP and ask them to design a play plan to go with that child and the parents/carers.
● Then ask them to role play the setting up of the play plan by one colleague playing the practitioner, one the child and one the parent or carer.
● The practitioner should demonstrate what to do to the parent or carer who should then practise with the child, using real equipment or resources. Explain that this makes it more likely that the play plan will be used confidently and effectively.
● Share your play plans and examples of the role play.
● Circulate the evaluation form and ask colleagues to complete it.

Our SEN Policy

Use this framework to develop an SEN policy for your setting, working with colleagues.

We believe that all children have a right to:
Our SEN Policy aims to:
Our special educational needs co-ordinator or 'SENCO' is called:
This is what our SENCO does:
We offer admission to all children who:
These members of staff have had training in SEN:
We currently receive this input from outside professionals:
We identify SEN by taking Early Years Action. This means:
We can request further support through Early Years Action Plus. This means:
We plan approaches for children with SEN in these ways:
These adaptations have been made to our premises to make them more accessible:
We monitor our SEN policy by:
Complaints about SEN provision should be made to the SENCO who will:
We attend SEN training regularly through:
We have these resources for SEN:
We keep parents and carers in touch with their child's progress through:
When a child with SEN transfers to another setting we:

Individual education plan

Photocopy the next two pages back-to-back

Name:

'Early Years Action/Plus/statemented'

My learning difficulty:

My strengths:

What I enjoy best:

What I need help with: (please ask me first!)

The action planned to support and include me:

Who will do what:

Help from my parents or carers:

Individual education plan (continued)

My targets:

1

2

3

4

How we will know I have been successful:

When the IEP will be reviewed:

Who will be invited to the review meeting:

SENCO consultation

Name of child:	Early Years Action/Plus	
Date of consultation:		
Who was present?		
What are the difficulties or needs you are worried about?		
What approaches have you tried so far?		
What effects have you noticed?		
How would you like things to change?		
Are there other factors you think might be important?		
How are parents or carers involved?		
What do parents or carers feel about the problem?		
Is any other agency involved?		
What will we do to meet the SEN of this child?		
Actions:	To be carried out by:	
When will we talk about this again?		

Special needs register

Child's name:

Name of setting:

Year:

Nature of concern:

Early Years Action/Plus/statement:

Date of initial meeting with carers:

First review date:

Second review date:

Third review date:

Outcome:

Invitation to review meeting

Our setting: Date:

Dear

As you know, we are planning ways of helping   to

make progress in our setting.

We would like to meet up to share how things are going and what we

are all doing to help.

Please could you come in to see us on:

Date: Time:

Place:

If this is not convenient, please contact us to find a better time.

We will also be inviting:

With many thanks

Yours sincerely

- -

Please return this slip as soon as you can:

I/we will/will not be able to attend the review meeting on:

Signed: (parent/guardian)

Carers' contribution to review meeting

Name of your child:

At home

When does your child need most help at home?

What does your child enjoy most at home?

Are there any changes at home we need to know about?

About the group

Is your child happy to come to the group?

Are you worried about anything to do with the group?

How do you feel about your child's progress?

Do you feel your child's needs are being met?

Health

How has your child's health been lately?

Are there any changes in medication or treatment?

The future

What would you like to see your child learning to do next?

Are you worried about anything in the future?

What questions would you like to ask at the review?

What changes would you like to see following the review?

Progress review

Early Years Action/Early Years Action Plus	
Name of Child: Who was present?	Date of Review meeting: Who has sent reports (attached):
Since we last met, this progress has been made:	
This is the special support which we have arranged so far:	
How helpful has this been?	
Are there any recent changes in the situation?	
Have the targets on the previous IEP been achieved?	
These are the targets we hope to see by the next review:	
This is the support we will arrange: (Negotiate and attach the current IEP)	
Date of next review meeting:	

My play plan

My name is	Date

Here is my target to do at home this week:

Games to play:

This is how my parent or carer will help me:

This is how we will know that I have been successful:

This is how I got on:

Joint planning meeting

Name of child: _____ Date of birth: _____

Address: _____

_____

_____ Setting: _____

Dear Colleague,

As you may know, this child is due to join our setting on: _____
We are holding an initial planning meeting to help us plan the best
approaches.

Day: _____ **Time:** _____ **Venue:** _____

The purposes of this meeting will be:

✎ to gather and share all relevant
information

✎ to hand over between professionals

✎ to help us to plan our approaches

✎ to learn about what approaches have
helped in the past

✎ to learn who can be called upon to
help in the future

✎ to set up good communication for the
future

✎ to reassure and support staff who will
be in direct contact with the child

✎ to address potential difficulties early on

✎ to detail the need for any specific
resources from outside the setting.

We do hope you can attend, or perhaps send us any information which
will be helpful. We are looking forward to welcoming this child and to
providing the best support we can.

Yours faithfully,

Hurray!

Today everyone was very proud of me because:

I was given a sticker each time and here they are:

Differentiation

Think through how you can make a play activity more accessible for a child with SEN. Perhaps you can:

- Make the play activity easier for the child?

- Offer more help, for example hand-over-hand, a point or a reminder?

- Reduce the distractions – sit in a quieter area or offer less choice?

- Play in a smaller group with an adult to support?

- Change the materials, such as stacking large blocks instead of small bricks?

- Expect slightly less of the child, for example, have a shorter story session?

- Plan more adult support – perhaps a 'shadow' during outdoor playtime?

- Build up the time gradually, for example, starting with only two minutes?

- Offer more adult support, perhaps a helper at listening time?

- Teach a new skill step by small step, that is, by breaking it down more?

- Make an activity more rewarding or exciting, for example, by cheering?

- Rearrange the equipment or spaces – try working at floor level?

Add your own ideas:

Step-by-step planning sheet

Name of Child:
Nature of difficulty:
Area of Learning:
Stepping Stone(s):
Target:

Steps along the way:		Date achieved
1		
2		
3		
4		
5		
6		

Resources and support needed:

Help from parents:

Choosing the right words

What you want to say	What you will say instead
Your child has a behaviour problem.	He enjoys himself a lot here and has a go at everything. We noticed that he finds it hard to share and quickly becomes upset if things don't go to plan – have you noticed this at home?
We think she's too solitary	We've noticed that she likes to be on her own a lot. Has she had much experience of being with other children?
Is she toilet-trained yet?	How much help does she need on the toilet?
He's got a speech problem.	
He's not coping and cries a lot.	
She's a slow learner.	
We don't think you help her enough.	
Stop threatening to smack him.	
His behaviour is odd.	
We think she can't hear clearly.	
Don't talk down to her all the time.	
He needs to see a psychologist.	
We don't think he'll cope in school.	

Use positive wording to complete the chart

Evaluation of SEN training

Please delete and answer as appropriate

Title of training event:
Presenter: Date:
The training session was too fast/about right/too slow
I liked:
I could have done without:
I could have done with more on:
The opportunity for discussion was too little/about right/too much The amount of small group work was too little/about right/too much Is there anything you would have liked to change?
At the end of the training, how are you feeling? bored/exhilarated/frustrated/stimulated/disheartened/more confident/puzzled/satisfied Anything else?
Is there anything else you would like to tell us about the training, the venue or the refreshments?   Thank you.

Resource list

Use this as a course handout.
Tick the books available in your setting

☐ DfES: *SEN Code of Practice* (ref DfES 581/2001)

☐ DfES: *SEN Toolkit* (ref DfES 558/2001)

☐ DfEE: *Full Day Care: National standards for under eights day care and childminding* (ref DfEE 0488/2001)

☐ *All Together: How to create inclusive services for disabled children and their families.* 2nd edition (National Children's Bureau, 8 Wakley Street, London EC1V 7QE, www.ncb.org.uk)

☐ 'Early Years and the Disability Discrimination Act 1995: What service providers need to know' produced by the Council for Disabled Children, Sure Start and the National Children's Bureau (NCB – see above)

☐ *Special needs in early years settings – A Guide for Practitioners* by Collette Drifte (David Fulton Publishers)

☐ *Toddler Taming: A Parent's Guide to the First Four Years* by Dr Christopher Green, Vermilion.

☐ *Special Needs and Early Years Provision* by Hannah Mortimer (Continuum)

☐ Scholastic *Special Needs in the Early Years* series – *Autistic spectrum difficulties, Behavioural and emotional difficulties, Essential A–Z guide to special needs, Learning difficulties, Medical difficulties, Physical and co-ordination difficulties, Sensory difficulties, Speech and language difficulties* and *Special Needs Handbook*

☐ *Special Needs and Early Years: A practitioner's guide* by Kate Wall (P. Chapman)

Add your own: